Deliverance:
A Survival Guide to
Parenting Twins

Deliverance:
A Survival Guide to
Parenting Twins

10 FIELD-TESTED TIPS TO NAVIGATE THE FIRST YEAR

Melinda L. Wentzel

aka Planet Mom

Planet Mom Publications
Caricature by Simon Ellinas

ISBN: 0692830014
ISBN 13: 9780692830017
Library of Congress Control Number: 2017930966
Planet Mom Publications, Williamsport, PA

For Seek and Destroy
Love you to the moon…and back.

Additional Praise For *Deliverance: A Survival Guide To Parenting Twins*

"The experts always talk about finding a balance when parenting. I quickly learned that when parenting twins, your world is more about the extremes. When faced with the choice of laughing or crying, choose to laugh while reading the honest truth only parents who are seeing double will understand in *Deliverance: A Survival Guide to Parenting Twins*." (Brooke Marie Beiter, embracing year three as a parent of twins and a singleton and a full-time job as a high school assistant principal, Williamsport, PA).

"In *Deliverance: A Survival Guide to Parenting Twins*, Melinda Wentzel hilariously proves once and for all that there are two things for which we are never prepared, and that is twins." (Robert Wilder, author of *Daddy Needs a Drink*, *Tales from the Teachers' Lounge* and *Nickel*, Santa Fe, NM).

"I have long been an admirer of Planet Mom and her heartfelt and personal explorations of parenting. Now, with her new book, *Deliverance: A Survival Guide to Parenting Twins*, she's not only going to be entertaining parents of twins, she's also going to be saving lives." (Garrett Rice, author of *Neanderdad*, San Mateo, CA).

"*Deliverance* delivers both laughs and advice, which makes it a twin win." (Jerry Zezima, syndicated humor columnist for The Stamford (Connecticut) Advocate and author of *Leave it to Boomer*, *The Empty Nest Chronicles* and *Grandfather Knows Best*, Suffolk County, NY).

"For anyone who's expecting twins, has twins, or even is about to welcome just one baby into their home, Melinda Wentzel's book, *Deliverance: A Survival Guide to Parenting Twins*, offers candid insights and valuable tips for new parents through her own hilarious and yes, sometimes exhausting experiences raising two screaming demons at one time." (Tracy Beckerman, nationally syndicated columnist and author, *Lost in Suburbia: A Momoir*, New Jersey).

Beckerman also added: "Your writing is smart, your experiences are totally relatable—not just to someone who's had twins, but anyone in the first year of motherhood—and your reflections on this experience are downright hilarious. I love what you've done here…"

"I've always been in awe of parents of multiples, and, especially after the newborn stage, I can definitely appreciate the feat of survival. Every time I read a portion of it, I always felt as if we'd shared a cup of coffee and heard the stories in person—which makes for a great read!" (Audrey Comerford, mom of a toddler and a newborn, Williamsport, PA).

"As a mom of twins, I believe *Deliverance* should be mandatory reading for all prospective parents of multiples. Planet Mom, you have completely captured the unique essence of rearing twins and your 10 field-tested tips are brilliant, sanity-saving nuggets of wisdom that make doubles doable and multiples manageable. Thanks for creating a real, raw, highly entertaining and informative road map to blaze the trail for new (soon-to-be-sleep-deprived-psychotic) parents of multiples." (Jennifer Cooley, mother of twins, Montoursville, PA).

Cooley also added: "Thanks so much for sharing the gift of *Deliverance* with me. Sorry for hoarding your amazing survival guide—I LOVED EVERY PAGE, laughed out loud, cried and wet my pants while reading your witty, hilarious pearls of wisdom!!!! My only regret is that I wish I had read your book BEFORE our 'twinadoes' came on the scene. (May have eliminated my need for a coffee IV and a valium salt lick)."

"A fun read for parents of twins who will relate to the sweet, funny and sometimes horrifying tales spun by Melinda, and an even better read for parents who don't have twins because they can see how easy they have it." (Wendi Aarons, award-winning humor writer, Austin, TX).

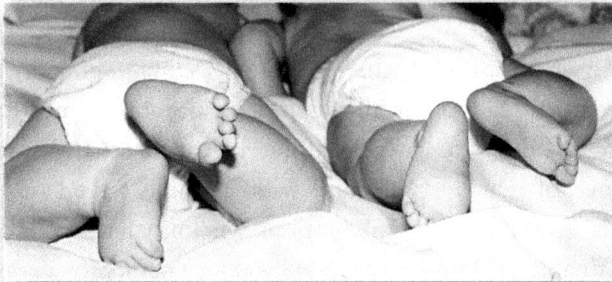

Contents

Additional Praise For *Deliverance:*
A Survival Guide To Parenting Twins · · · · · · · vii

Preface · xv

Chapter 1   Sleep When They Sleep, You Damn Fool. · · · 1

Chapter 2   Swallow Your Pride—Accept Help. · · · · · · 7

Chapter 3   Stop Stressing About Your Hideous Belly. · · 13

Chapter 4   Adopt the Assembly Line Mentality.

Or Die. · 19

Chapter 5   Shower and Brush Your Teeth. Please. · · · · 27

Chapter 6   Find Your Tribe. · · · · · · · · · · · · · · · · · 33

Chapter 7   Make it a Double. · · · · · · · · · · · · · · · · 41

Chapter 8   Twin Fascination is Real. Brace Yourself. · · 47

Chapter 9   Romance for Dummies. · · · · · · · · · · · · · 55

Chapter 10 Get in Gear. · 63

             Epilogue · 73

             DELIVERANCE QUIZ · · · · · · · · · · · · · · · 81

             DELIVERANCE QUIZ ANSWERS · · · · · · · 85

             About the Author · · · · · · · · · · · · · · · · · 89

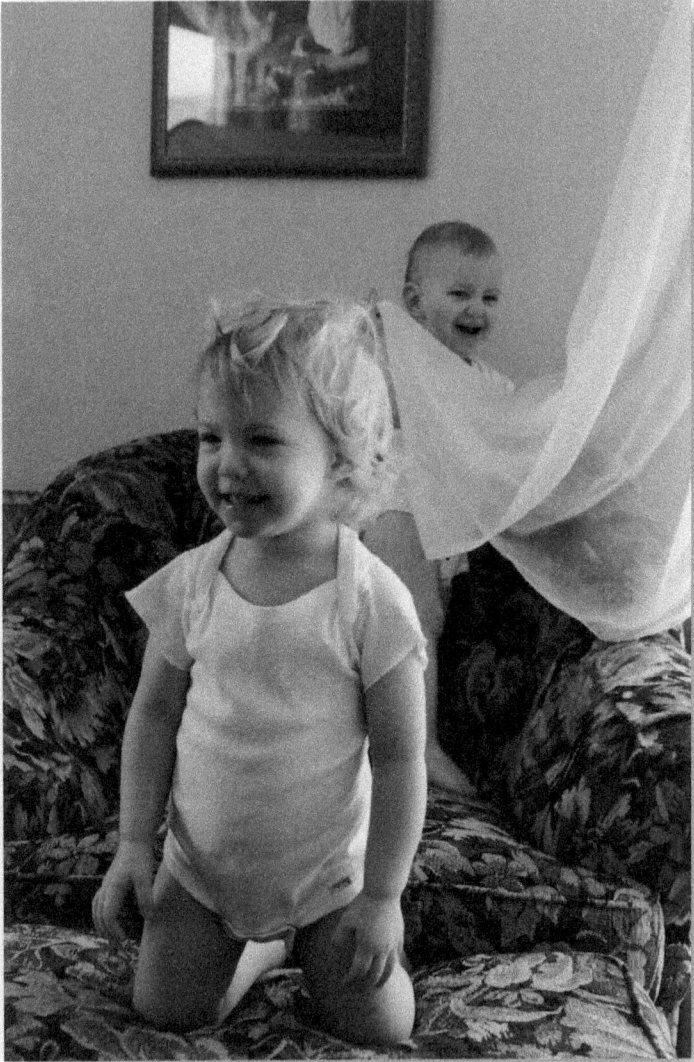

Preface

B abies are insanely demanding, yet profoundly love-able creatures. They render us incapable of rational thought and the ability to function without sway-ing with an armload of groceries—or potting soil—or biodegradable cat litter—or practically anything, actually. Like pint-sized parcels of warmth and fuzziness soused in that which is sweet and extraordinary, infants capture our hearts, seize our souls and satisfy our every desire for pur-pose in this life.

Almost.

That said, the vat of things that went wrong when my husband and I returned home from the hospital with our doll-sized twins fairly obliterated any and all visions I had had of the perfect homecoming. Our five-pound bundles of neediness had, quite ceremoniously, arrived early. Translation: I suffered from preeclampsia and was about two heartbeats away from an exciting helicopter ride to the nearest hospital with a Neonatal Intensive Care Unit, which meant that our nursery wasn't even close to being ready, our freakishly large car seats were entirely impracticable and we had stockpiled exactly *zero* preemie-sized diapers. Diapers so small they could have been worn by malnourished guinea pigs. Or incontinent squirrels. Possibly both.

Furthermore, none of the clothing that had been so graciously bestowed upon us in the weeks and months leading up to THE BIG DAY actually fit the smallish beings who would soon command our every thought, word and deed. So we improvised with doll clothes for a time. Seriously. We did this.

Stop laughing.

Worse yet, neither of us possessed the intellect or patience required to assemble the monstrosity-of-a-playpen/bassinet that mocked our every effort—the blue-checkered cube of doom that would eventually become the focal point of our living-room-turned-shrine-to-impressionable-youth.

So we just stood there. Like asshats. Having no place to safely set the aforementioned bundles of neediness, stupidly gawking at one another as if we each held an unwieldy sack of potatoes. Sacks that were, of course, shrouded in two of the most ~~obscenely expensive~~ adorable outfits on the planet. Knitted wonders that beckoned to us unremittingly from the hospital gift shop on the morning we checked out. Had we been remotely lucid, we would have purchased volumes of ridiculously small diapers, too, strapping them to the roof of the minivan I would grow to despise. But by the time we arrived home and stood in our living room, the point was decidedly moot. Lucidity would not come to call for a very long time.

So we then swayed back and forth, in a futile yet fervent attempt to keep our writhing infants from waking, completely and perhaps justifiably terrified of what might happen should they begin to wail. The team of NICU nurses—and the safety net they had so widely cast beneath our sorry souls for two solid weeks—was gone. Needless to say, I had grown inordinately dependent upon their vigilant presence and constant assurances that everything was fine, that *all* preemies become exhausted and scream like banshees when bathed, that eventually my less-than-functional breasts would produce voluminous quantities of milk, that mothering twins wouldn't prove to be a horrific, soul sucking affair, that my babies were breathing—and breathing was good.

Naturally, I allowed waves of panic and a healthy dose of irrational fear to consume me, running through the gamut of all that could possibly go wrong in the days, weeks and years to come. What if our cats carry them away in the night? What if they swallow their comically oversized pacifiers? What if they join a cult, tattoo something ludicrous upon their foreheads or marry someone with a mullet? What if we never figure out how to put this fucking playpen together and we spend the rest of our miserable lives standing right here in this godforsaken room?

For the record, we assembled the not-so-endearing playpen that day with the help of a non-judgy neighbor and eventually became liberated from the confines of our living room. The past sixteen years, though inundated with more rage-filled moments than I'd care to admit, have been nothing less than a whirlwind of joy and a boundless source of that which is memorable and good. It's been richly edifying as well, involving an abundance of missteps and an abiding allegiance to the art of muddling through. The guide you now hold in your hands is a byproduct of that allegiance— a shamelessly candid and exceedingly palpable tale of survival as it were. Proof positive that I somehow managed the first year of mothering twins—without nannies, without sedatives and without becoming completely unhinged—for more than three days running, anyway.

It is, in effect, the deliverance I sought as I wended my way over the uncertain path and through the tangled wood of parenting two—who, again and again, demanded *all of me* in the very same instant. That said, there are exactly 10 crucial bits of information you need to know about raising twins in the first year and I've assembled them here on the pages that follow. Take heed, take heart and tie your sneakers, buttercup. There *will* be a quiz.

CHAPTER 1

Sleep When They Sleep, You Damn Fool.

I n the beginning, there were interminable stretches of time, centuries maybe, during which I would have given anything for a solid night of sleep. And by anything, I submit to you that that list might have included my firstborn child, my genuine Thurman Munson baseball card (circa 1977) or my left kidney, which had been beaten into submission during the pregnancy from hell anyway. So it had, in effect, already been sacrificed to the gods of conception.

For all intents and purposes, sleep was deemed a priceless commodity during the first year with my twins, one that I craved with a ferocity beyond all imagining. So I did what any sensible person would do. I dozed unabashedly at every opportunity that befell me—mostly because I was entirely incapable of remaining conscious. That said, I napped at stoplights and at story time in the musty basement of our public library. At school functions and on the sidelines of soccer fields while my oldest frolicked in the mud. I even nodded off while seated in profoundly uncomfortable church pews and while holed up in a number of waiting rooms teeming with petulant children and/or flea-bitten dogs and cats. I even had the audacity to sneak upstairs for a reprieve from mom duty once or twice while visitors had dropped by unannounced—which was completely juvenile now that I think about it, yet wholly essential to my sanity. "It wasn't *me* they came to see anyway," I rationalized. "And besides, I haven't showered in three days, so basically I'm doing everyone a favor."

My husband, too, was desperate for sleep. The mere suggestion of it made him heady with the prospect. As one might expect, he often crashed at work as a high school principal having been up half the night ferrying babies hither and yon and channel surfing for pretty much anything and everything that would inspire a wakeful state. Naturally, my husband hoped and prayed that co-workers wouldn't notice the disjointed nature of his speech during meetings and whatnot the following day. It's rumored that his brain went on hiatus in mid-afternoon. Usually in mid-sentence. Sadly, I wasn't there to witness his stupor firsthand. Instead I had to settle for hearing about his journey to the land of incoherence from those who were entertained by his condition. The list was many.

Indeed, our collective desire for shuteye was categorically off the charts. Case in point: At a time when our progenies were very small, we (i.e. just the two of us) spent a 24-hour chunk of deliciousness in a massively opulent hotel room—a honeymoon suite more specifically, one equipped with a gargantuan hot tub and wet bar—sleeping. Yes, SLEEPING. After a filling meal and roughly eight minutes of idle conversation, we fell into a deep, coma-inspired sleep in the tub, sudsy water lapping at our chins. We were supposed to paint the town six shades of red later that evening, not once thinking of our dear children. We were supposed to indulge ourselves and each other—to reconnect as a couple over fine cuisine and sinful quantities of alcohol. We were supposed to engage in endless sessions of wanton sex, pausing only to reflect on its impracticality in a hot tub. But it was not to be. The siren song of sleep was calling, as it always did during that unforgettable first year.

In hindsight, we would have been wise to listen to our impossibly fatigued bodies on a regular basis (not to mention the swarming masses who freely shared with us how utterly deplorable we looked). We should have seized the opportunities (fleeting though they might have been) for rest—to sleep while the babies slept. Morning, noon and night.

Like idiots, we rarely did this. Instead, we felt compelled to watch bad TV and to phone eleventy-seven of our closest friends, to scrub toilets and sort laundry, to vacuum and dust, to taxi our oldest the world over and to snap a profusion of photos featuring the smallish beings who had rocked our proverbial world. Stuff that wasn't imperative to our day-to-day functioning. Stuff that many of our trusted friends and family had offered to do *for* us. Stuff to which we stubbornly clung for fear of losing our tenuous grip on the vestiges of control, which was a fool's errand in every sense of the phrase.

God knows we got the merest suggestion of sleep during that first year. As newish parents, we lived in a chaos-filled, baby-saturated world where it seemed as though everything related to self-preservation was an afterthought. But somehow we managed to recognize the importance of being kind to ourselves despite the fact that it was a tremendously tall order. Like so many people who beat themselves unmercifully for not being good enough, we were easy targets for criticism, which made the tenet that much harder to uphold.

We also tried desperately to be flexible, to laugh at ourselves often and to keep things in proper perspective when frustration or panic would darken our door. That said, I called my mom roughly 648 times with the first baby, completely distraught by umbilical cord awfulness, crib diving and anything else that I couldn't possibly handle like a rational person; so I endeavored to do less of that with subsequent offspring. Another tall order.

What's more, my husband and I recognized how crucial it was to reprioritize our lives, at least in the short term, and to know our limitations. Hosting a party for 50 of our closest friends during that initial year wasn't even in the realm of possibility—and we knew it. Making home movies—documenting our children's growth and the journey we made as a family—was far more meaningful in the end. Needless to say, the videos served as a constant reminder that change was afoot, and that we had better not blink.

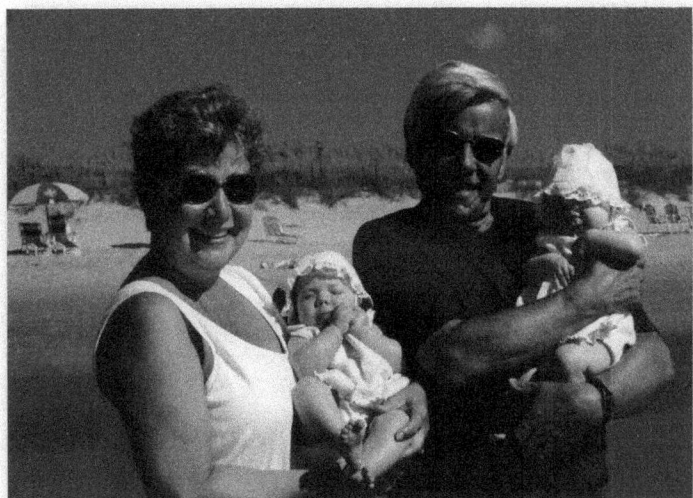

CHAPTER 2

Swallow Your Pride—Accept Help.

For a long time I was too proud to ask anyone for anything that might have made my life the least bit easier. I worried about being judged in the short term as a parent of newborn twins, and about being branded as a colossal failure for life. Worse yet, I feared becoming dependent on others and envisioned the resulting guilt I would duly harbor as intolerable. Furthermore, I wasn't especially fond of the idea of having people in my house—people who would likely fold my unmentionables, count the pizza boxes stacked in my garage and discover the shameful abundance of dust that lurked behind my refrigerator—never mind the fetid masses that surely lurked *inside* my refrigerator. Besides, there was always the very real possibility that my husband's socks would be mismatched or that my breast milk might mistakenly wind up in someone's damned omelet.

Despite all logic and understanding, if the aforementioned kindly individuals offered to care for our children so I that might ~~avoid a meltdown of epic proportions~~ fetch a loaf of bread without the hassle of car seats et al., somehow I'd resent their presence (i.e. for having robbed me of a golden opportunity—like changing someone's 247th diaper, dealing with simultaneous bouts of colic or scraping warm clumps of cat vomit from the carpet while I was away). Lord knows how I love stumbling upon the fresh hell that is cat puke, so missing the chance to extract said vileness from my carpet fibers would have, indeed, been a disappointment.

Needless to say, I had issues with delegating responsibility and with the notion of accepting help altogether; but eventually I swallowed my pride and came to terms with the reality that I couldn't manage entirely on my own. That's code for: I feared I would implode the very next time I wrestled with a diaper pail and lost. My husband, too, recognized this undeniable truth, having acknowledged that we desperately needed the support of others on occasion.

Looking back, there were so many wonderful people who did so many wonderful things in the name of preserving our collective sanity. People who mowed our lawn and gathered our mail, shopped for groceries and scrubbed our sinks, proffered all manner of must-have-infant-gear and, thankfully, helped us build insanely complicated baby paraphernalia lest we commit hari-kari in the process of attempting to construct it ourselves. What's more, they cooked some of the most delectable meals we've ever consumed and cared for our children as if they were their own. It's rumored they hauled several metric tons of poo to the curbside with glee, washed an inordinate number of filthy windows and folded an embarrassment of laundry (in a grossly improper manner, I might add), and yet I cannot adequately express how profoundly appreciative I was then and continue to be now.

In retrospect, it would have made perfect sense to compile a comprehensive list of the ways in which people could've legitimately helped—a detailed and shameless collection of duties and odd jobs that I had no qualms about outsourcing (i.e. necessary stuff that I wasn't necessarily able to accomplish without divine intervention and six more sets of hands). People could've simply scrawled their names next to the task they wanted to complete, along with a time or date to avoid any confusion. Conversely, whenever friends and family spontaneously inquired as to providing assistance, invariably, I suffered from a sudden and incapacitating lapse of coherent thought—a veritable fugue-like state in which I was unable to reliably produce my name, let alone a three-word suggestion like: WATER THE PLANTS. Sadly, and as a result, several plants were, indeed, harmed in the rearing of the children in question.

Had I been clever enough to craft such a list and subsequently coordinate the efforts of those willing to sign on, I have no doubt that that first year would have been markedly less stressful for my husband and me (not to mention, for the ill-fated plants). Well, the process of managing the good deed doers would have been more orderly anyway, and we could have avoided the idiocy of having 17 people show up to change the cat box on the same day. Likewise, I could have (and should have) composed a list of individuals willing to be contacted at any hour of the day or night in order to step in and help me—a cavalry of sorts, that would've made themselves readily available in the event of an end-of-my-proverbial-rope type of emergency, no questions asked. Just knowing that a team of rescuers was there would've relieved a great deal of my anxiety.

I would've been wise to call on friends or family when I got sick, too. Instead I remember toughing it out, trying to care for two of the neediest creatures on the planet when I felt only slightly better than road kill myself. Then, too, when our entire family was stricken with the latest plague, the conditions were very nearly insufferable. I'm sure I was mired by guilt, and therefore refused to contact anyone who might be in a position to offer assistance. Needless to say, I dabble and sometimes dance with idiocy.

Thankfully I *was* bright enough to take someone with me to help with pediatrician's visits. Otherwise, I have no idea how I would've managed. Getting to and from the office while hauling a diaper bag, purse and both babies, would've been a supreme challenge, let alone dealing with the whole immunization nightmare on my own.

At any rate, it's important to understand that parenting isn't some sort of glorified contest wherein the degree of difficulty is factored in for various assignments, and gold stars are awarded at the end for effort. Twenty or thirty years from now no one's going to give a damn that your closets were impeccably organized or that everything fit neatly into your garage throughout the entire span of childrearing. If that's the case, by the way, I hate you. Furthermore, there is no glory in martyrdom and no shame in allowing others to lend a hand—especially during that incredibly challenging first year.

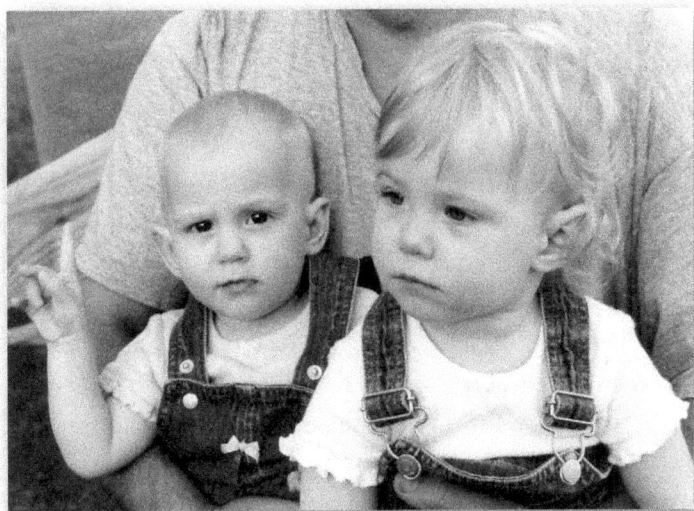

CHAPTER 3

Stop Stressing About Your Hideous Belly.

S top stressing about your hideous belly. Seriously. Stop doing that. It's unhealthy. And besides, your belly isn't all that hideous anyway. Trust me. I've seen hideous. That's code for: I've gasped audibly upon viewing my reflection in the mirror, pausing like a jackass so that I might indelibly imprint said horror upon my mind for all eternity. On a related note, please don't send me snapshots involving any part of your anatomy, past or present. I will thank you in advance.

As one might expect, I became disturbingly obsessed with my abdomen throughout my twin pregnancy, especially during the last trimester as my womb grew freakishly large in what seemed like hourly increments. In a word, it was an unparalleled source of fascination for one and all. And by one and all, I mean my immediate family and the visitors who were foolish enough to drop by unannounced as I lay on the couch, my bare midriff protruding toward the heavens like some sort of Himalayan topography gone wrong. Because it moved. My belly, that is. In the spirit of tsunamis and sci-fi flicks, sudden surges (i.e. flashes of tiny knees and elbows) as well as undulating swells of softball-sized whateverness (read: movements that I'm certain corresponded to in utero summersaults and/or exorcism) seized my midsection, rendering onlookers wholly entranced and perfectly horrified. Needless to say, we didn't regularly attend the circus at the time. We didn't need to. I *was* the freak show.

Aside from inadvertently whacking everything in my path with my obscenely pregnant self, and engaging in the idiocy that involves bending over to retrieve the sixty bazillion items I dropped on the floor during that wedge of gestational joy, I also spent a goodly portion of time holed up in the shower, ogling my Hindenburg-inspired abdomen. That is not to say that my stomach was oblong or imbued with hydrogen by any stretch. Just massive. And unwieldy. Much like a planet, tethered to the very essence of density. That said, my girth was intolerable, frighteningly surreal and offensive to my sensibilities. Indeed, it sought to crush my soul each and every time I stood in the shower, unable to see my cussed feet. Quite literally, the elephant in the room.

Eventually, I found the not-being-able-to-see-my-feet thing amusing in the very same way that I thought being paralyzed from the waist down for my first C-section was positively hilarious. Strange, but true. After a time, however, both circumstances became increasingly unsettling, causing me to hover on the fringe of dread on more than one occasion. "What if my toes sprout peacock feathers and no one tells me?" (I considered, thoroughly consumed by one of many irrational fears in the latter months of my pregnancy). "What if the hospital becomes engulfed in flames during surgery and you somehow forget to wheel me outside?" I actually inquired of the OR staff.

Apparently, there's a moron in every crowd. One, in particular, fixated upon fire and feathers.

It's not as if there weren't other reminders of my immensity, though. Like the fact that I had to *lift* my belly in order to roll over in bed, and my grossly distorted belly button, for instance—the abhorrent bulge at my core that became the curious focus of so many awkward exchanges. Even with strangers. Perhaps *especially* with strangers— ones who probably likened the unsightly stub of flesh lurking beneath my tent-of-a-shirt to a third nipple or to the herniated neck of a sad little balloon, turned inside out against its will. Granted, it's difficult to ignore something so strikingly obvious—not to mention repulsive, like so many failed attempts to avert one's eyes from a grocery clerk's less-than-lovely tongue piercing. It's virtually impossible not to gawk, let alone ask a series of tactless questions. So it's understandable that people might want to discuss a misshapen and decidedly odd navel and/or a barn-sized belly. Sort of.

Making matters worse, I had outgrown most of my maternity clothes by the seventh month, forever altering the integrity of my husband's t-shirts (a transgression for which I still harbor a modicum of guilt). As a result, I felt horrible, and huge—never mind undesirable. Not to be confused with the day I discovered that I could no longer wedge the enormity of my midsection between the seat and steering wheel of our SUV, assuming I might also want to reach the pedals so I could drive anywhere. The crowning blow was the shocking realization that the seat belt flatly refused to span the swell of my stomach, making a mockery of my waistline. So I did what any impossibly pregnant woman would do—I retreated to the living room and planted my sorry self on the couch, a tub of small curd cottage cheese at my side, the remote control hermetically sealed to my hand, a small white flag hoisted above my head in surrender.

There was yet another friendly reminder of my larger-than-life-sized frame that occurred the morning after I had given birth. A hospital worker had stopped by to empty the trash and to take the remnants of my charred toast back to the kitchen. While clearing my tray she asked with far more cheer than I could ably handle after an exhausting night, "So when are you due, Hon?" Of course, this fueled a crying jag that wouldn't stop, very nearly eclipsing the utter despair and defeat I felt after a ~~mean and horrible troll-of-a-man~~ male nurse callously suggested that I was a poster child for breastfeeding failure. Well, not in so many words. But the implication was there, effectively sending me the message that it was best to give up on the idea of nursing altogether, planting the seed that I would surely starve my children by trying. A real joy bringer. I secretly hoped the electric breast pumping machine that lived in the little room next to the nurse's station would go rogue one day, just as the aforementioned jerk strolled by, swallowing him whole—beginning, of course, with his stony, insensitive heart.

In any event, I finally made peace with a world sprinkled with inconsiderate people and with my size, embracing every inch of my behemoth belly all in the name of creating babies I would later deem more wonderful than life itself.

CHAPTER 4

Adopt the Assembly Line Mentality. Or Die.

think it's fair to say that I'm one of those people who goes through life doing things the hard way initially or, at the very least, doing things in a manner that is less than ideal. It builds character, I'm told. Like countless others, I've had the distinct advantage of looking back upon my poor decisions and botched practices so that I might examine them more closely, under the lens of clearheadedness and objectivity. Handling the daily affairs of two indescribably needy people with a binky dependency was no exception.

Case in point: Each time I did something exceedingly stupid, such as allowing Seek and Destroy to climb to the top of their very first flight of stairs SIMULTANEOUSLY without first teaching them how to back down one step at a time, I learned a valuable lesson—that panic is my least favorite motherly sentiment, one I'd like to avoid whenever possible. Granted, I did lots of things as a parent that could be construed as daft, but because the gods were smiling upon me much of the time I benefitted from the learning curve. In particular, I found that my mistakes related to time management (i.e. handling my twins' daily care needs like feeding, dressing, changing and bathing, in addition to our stunningly imperfect bedtime routine) eventually led to the development of a better system—one that would leave me feeling slightly more energized than a piece of driftwood by day's end.

Needless to say, at the start I invested a great deal of time and energy going through the motions of addressing each baby's individual needs, literally bouncing from one impossible demand to the next, my head reeling by the time I was faced with the dreaded task of putting my brood to bed. It seemed as though the very moment I finished cleaning up after changing someone's diaper, another mustard-hued gift was deposited in someone else's pants. Joy. Ultimately, I learned the value of at least checking the second diaper. Similarly, after having fed one child, the next would begin to wail with gusto. Goat-like. And so it went, minute by minute, hour after hour, each tiny disaster merging seamlessly into the next. At the height of the madness, I remember being unable to readily recall which baby

I had just fed or changed—which meant that I was a more pathetic parent than I had previously considered possible. Admittedly, it felt as if I were drowning much of the time, unable to paddle hard enough to keep my head above water.

Finally I wised up enough to devise a makeshift record-keeping system for feedings and diaper changes, and also to employ a method historically perfected in the automobile industry by Henry Ford, the Assembly Line King. Once I recognized the beauty and simplicity of this marvelous plan, I applied it to nearly every situation I encountered with the dear waifs in question. That way, I only needed to gather the supplies (for bathing, dressing, diaper changing, feeding, etc.) once. Better still, only one cleanup was required.

Efficiency was my new superpower.

More specifically, I could bathe (dress, feed, change) one twin while the other was otherwise engaged in some sort of activity nearby (i.e. safely and completely contained within an age-appropriate apparatus designed to entertain). On a related note, our playpen/bassinet doubled as a changing table and it was particularly useful for diaper duty since I could set one twin's dirty diaper *inside* the playpen (and out of reach) on a disposable cloth while the other twin was free to crawl around within eyeshot in a secure area of our home (more expressly: NOT EATING POO

OR DECORATING THE WALLS WITH IT). After the task at hand was finished, I'd switch the babies and high-five myself for being so damned clever.

What's more, I discovered that some things could be accomplished more effectively if carried out at the exact same moment in time, like nursing (using a twin nursing pillow) and/or bottle-feeding. Eventually, I invested in a twin bouncer, color-coded the bottles and let them feed themselves. Moreover, I remembered and actually used a lot of the information that my lactation consultant (more affectionately known as The Boob Guru) imparted during my hospital stay, perfecting several different nursing positions over time, saving a ton of money and untold hours in the process. Additionally, her advice was extraordinarily helpful when I suffered from a nasty bout of mastitis, aka Hell Week.

Arguably the most intelligent use of the assembly line mentality involved putting our kids to bed roughly three nanoseconds apart (on a good night)—after we successfully Ferberized them, that is. Initially, my husband and I allowed our world to be governed by the aforementioned children, caving in to their collective desire to be read 746 books each night on average, then rocked to sleep, placed in their cribs, their backs gently patted as we lay on the nursery room floor, our arms twisted unmercifully through the rungs so that we could continue said patting for an un-determined period of time (translation: fucking forever).

So we turned to Dr. Richard Ferber's sleep training method at the sage advice of our pediatrician, who had not-so-subtly suggested that my sleep starved appearance was beyond piteous and fast approaching dreadful. As much as I appreciated his candor (not especially), I dis-covered that I was wholly incapable of carrying out the famed regimen once it became evident that I'd have to listen to my progenies wail for what seemed like an eter-nity—night after night, until they learned to self-soothe and eventually fall asleep without my constant presence. *Oh, the horror.*

So I stood in the garage, a failed baby whisperer, while my husband carried out the deed with little or no difficul-ty—a man's man. I stood in the garage because, of course, my children's cries couldn't be heard there. Naturally, I al-lowed the full gamut of my imagination to take root in my psyche, filling me with torment and dread as it related to how things were going in the nursery. Of all my motherly skills, it is without a shred of doubt my shining star.

In the end, our twins learned to put themselves to sleep and we were able to add that to the growing list of things we could accomplish using the assembly line technique. It followed that we put them on the same schedule for virtually everything.

I'm pretty sure I'd be batshit crazy by now had we not succeeded in that endeavor. Another practice that saved us in so many ways was to divide and conquer. If only for a few minutes a day at home, my husband and I spent some quality time with each child (reading books, playing peek-a-boo, giving a bath, etc.) one-on-one. On occasion, usually a weekend, we split the pair and took them on errands around town, sharing the burden as well as opening the door of opportunity for individual bonding with each twin. It's a custom we continue to use and benefit from today, giving us ample time to celebrate their differences and matchless personalities. Without a doubt, it's time well spent.

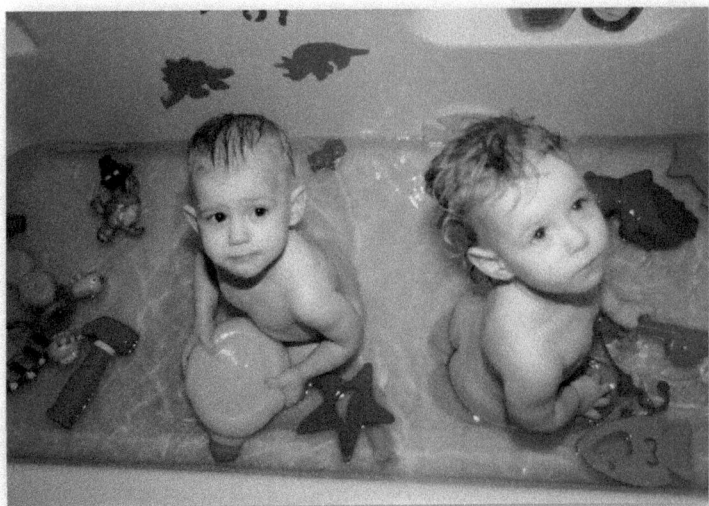

CHAPTER 5

Shower and Brush Your Teeth. Please.

There's nothing about parenthood that I enjoy more than not being able to shower regularly. Said no parent ever. I wasn't especially fond of redefining—as luxuries—that which I considered to be a modest collection of inalienable rights either, granted simply because I was human (i.e. brushing my teeth and using the toilet whenever I pleased, eating a real sit-down meal with something other than plastic silverware at least once daily or taking an uninterrupted nap on a Saturday afternoon, just because). But that's exactly what happened when I became a mother. The above-mentioned entitlements became indulgences; something I realized on rare occasions when the universe allowed it, aligning itself in such a manner that I might catch a break.

Little did I know that having a baby, or a set of twins, would feel remarkably akin to a bad camping trip—an ungainly foray into the woods involving far too little sleep and far too much gear, as well as an unhealthy fixation on the comforts of home or the lack thereof. Before children, I had fond remembrances of being able to leisurely attend to my basic needs, unfettered by anyone or anything. Parenthood had, in effect, carved out a new reality for me—one that entailed roughing it most days, as well as tripping over baby gates and wrestling with car seats. With regard to the metaphorical camping trip, it was the equivalent of stuffing my entire family inside a tiny, smelly tent, each of us trying (and failing) to make the "unkempt look" somehow trendy, sporting stale clothes and even staler breath for days on end.

Eventually I grew tired of that gritty feeling, so I devised a plan for dealing with my situation, intolerable as it seemed. As one might expect, baby gear came to the rescue. In order to grab a quick shower, or to carry out pretty much any toiletry-related endeavor, I placed my cherubs within two age-appropriate gadgets intended to entertain. A twin bouncer worked well until they could climb out of it and crawl away, ~~ostensibly on the hunt for booze or something with which to light the house on fire~~. Swings were quite effective, too, except they were difficult to cart around and not especially well suited for the confines of anyone's bathroom.

I remember the best combination being a doorway jumper that some dear friends had loaned us and a godsend-of-an-activity-center, decked out with a tractor, a handful of farm animals and a silo that doubled as a thrilling chute for the farmer, his wife and the aforementioned barnyard animals. This was all well and good, of course, until Frick and Frack started amusing themselves by hurling the chickens across the room and at each other. What's more, they eventually exceeded the weight limits of said wonder toys and we had to re-strategize. Again.

But before that happened, I was able to rely on two age-appropriate devices by positioning them in close proximity to me—usually within the very same room—after I had checked/changed both diapers and completely ensured that the children in question would be safe for the duration. My only other option was to leave them in their cribs and worry they'd take a nosedive while I was in the shower (a very real possibility, given their thirst for adventure). As a last resort, I set my alarm and planned to wake before they did, allowing enough time to do what I needed to do, sacrificing my beloved sleep—an alternative I loathed with every ounce of my being.

In hindsight, I wish I had worked out the logistics of this matter in my head before I was faced with the problem, so that I wouldn't have had to sacrifice so much of what embodied self-preservation for me. It sounds a bit theatrical now, but I remember feeling defeated and incapable—desperate, almost, for a solution regarding an issue that for so many others was a non-issue. On a side note, I recognized with certainty that feeling bitter was not one of my more endearing qualities, nor did it make me a better parent.

The irony here, of course, was that I couldn't effectively manage a problem that I was unable to fully comprehend or envision—because it hadn't surfaced in my world yet. So much of mothering twins is like that. I didn't know it would be next to impossible to consume 96 fluid ounces of water a day, the recommended volume for breastfeeding success (and/or camel status), until I was met with the challenge head-on. I had no idea one of my greatest difficulties would be dealing with raw, cracked hands, ravaged from the constant scrubbing of bottles, changing of diapers and bathing of babies. I couldn't imagine how complicated it would be to maneuver my twins out of their car seats and into a store all by myself because I hadn't encountered the very real dilemma of not having enough hands away from home yet—nor did I entertain the notion that strollers aren't practical in every situation.

Thankfully I was able to brainstorm and experiment my way through this incredibly memorable phase of parenthood, realizing along the way a series of small victories. But initially, when I was home alone with my babies all I longed for was a hot shower, three squares and enough sleep to keep me sane. Months later, somewhere deep inside that unforgettable first year, I craved something more—a teensy block of *me time* that I could claim as my very own and consume in any way, shape or form that I desired (think: books, hobbies, socializing, exercise and/or a much-deserved deep tissue massage). And because my husband recognized how important such liberation was to me ~~how deranged I might become lest I be denied said wedge of freedom~~, he made it happen, structuring within his schedule a time for baby wrangling, so that I might reconnect with myself or with friends. He often suggested that I "…needed to get out with taller people" (which was entirely true).

Being able to bathe, eat and sleep with an element of expectation and predictability made me feel human. Being able to enjoy *me time* made me feel loved. Strive for both.

CHAPTER 6

Find Your Tribe.

Misery loves company. That is not to say that I was exceedingly miserable as a parent of newborn twins. It's just that during particularly trying times, when I *was* patently miserable, I enjoyed the company of others. More specifically, people who completely understood my woes and refrained from passing judgment. Even when it was apparent that I was certifiable. And haggardly.

Fortunately, I found that exact brand of compassion and solidarity within a local Parents of Multiples Club. But when it was first suggested that I join a support group for people like me I scoffed at the idea, foolishly thinking I didn't need anyone's empathy, nor did I need to add another event to my already overloaded calendar. After months of sleepless nights and endless days filled with glaring examples of my ineptitude as a mother of twins, however, I came to the realization that perhaps I *could* benefit from a meeting. Or twenty.

Almost instantly I was welcomed into the fold, embraced by an assemblage of parents bent on helping me succeed in spite of myself. Parents who knew what it was like to become unglued over a sitter that cancels at the last minute or a bout of projectile vomiting. Parents who nodded in agreement, sharing my pain when I bemoaned our 96-diaper-a-week habit. Mothers who bonded over nipple confusion and a scourge of stretch marks.

I had found my tribe.

Needless to say, my decision to fraternize with such people was one of my finest. Case in point: Veteran members taught me a host of valuable lessons such as: DON'T FEED THE TROLLS. Translation: Don't invite advice from strangers. They also pointed out the wisdom of designating one day a week to cook a bunch of meals ahead and freeze them, and to prepackage snacks in little bags so I could grab and go throughout my hectic day. My husband willingly volunteered his time and talents to carry out such a loving act, which quite literally saved me from myself.

What's more, and as a matter of course, the group encouraged members not only to unload the intimate details of their baggage within the sanctity of friends, but to individually unwrap each nugget of angst, indignation and regret, waving it above their heads, warts and all, until it no longer had the power to demoralize and dishearten. It was a remarkably cathartic experience to say the very least.

Naturally, we sought to connect over the good stuff, too, sharing the hilarity of each day with twins in tow and the indescribable joy they had brought to our lives. There was nothing quite like hearing someone's story firsthand, telling of their twins' desire to hold each other's hands or to converse with one another in a language only they could understand. "Twinspeak" was one of many new buzzwords I added to my vocabulary. What's more, I heard varying perspectives on hot button issues in education—something that wasn't pressing at the time, but would come to affect me eventually. Together we aired our common concerns and brainstormed for ideas to manage the problems that we, and others apparently, had encountered. Indeed, gathering once a month with such a likeminded bunch was both informative and uplifting. Sort of like our Lamaze class without all the heavy breathing.

Most importantly, joining a twins support group meant never having to feel alone in my frustration, my sleep-starved existence or in a world that felt as if it would be forever encumbered by diaper bags and baby gear. There was comfort in numbers and a certain degree of assurance in knowing that others had passed this way before.

They made it out alive. And so would I.

I remember the meetings as a newcomer feeling much like I had envisioned a 12-Step AA session would be—learning to cope amidst a myriad of challenges. After admitting that our lives had become decidedly unmanageable, we sought the refuge of those who could best understand, together confessing our deepest, darkest fear: not that we might use again, but that we'd pack our bags with peanut butter sandwiches and run away from home like an enraged eight-year-old, never again having to double our pleasure with colic or to deal with back-to-back three a.m. feedings. Regarding our overall mission to help each other navigate some of life's most difficult paths, I'm not sure our differences were all that great.

Not surprisingly, finding the underlying humor of parenthood helped, and because of the group atmosphere, it was that much more colorful, inviting even the most reluctant of participants. The more the merrier, as it were. That said, it was infinitely more amusing to hear about someone else's train wreck involving tandem teething and a complete loss of composure than it was to live through it personally (i.e. losing one's shit because our progenies wouldn't stop biting each other in a church pew). There was some measure of thrill, too, in competing for the Awful Award (read: a hypothetical grand prize granted to the teller of the most shocking, horrific, riotous, fill-in-the-blank tale involving the smallish beings in question). I came close to winning once when I confessed to having left my twins in the garage. They were sleeping soundly in their car seats while I unloaded the groceries. After I finished, I sat on the living room couch. BECAUSE I FORGOT I HAD CHILDREN. Momentarily.

In truth, support meetings were like glorified play dates for adults. Some of the parents of older twins would offer to give the newbies a break, occupying our infants while we engaged with others over the remains of the day and a plate full of chocolate chip cookies. What's more, as our children grew they discovered a host of playmates nestled within that close-knit group, some of whom were at developmentally similar stages—a win-win situation. We went on exciting field trips together, too, outings that were planned and orchestrated by our fearless leaders (i.e. den mothers). Good times were had by all.

As an added bonus, we found new homes for a wealth of baby gear and clothing we had outgrown. There was no need to advertise on a grand scale when the very people who might be interested in the aforementioned items could potentially walk through the door at the next meeting.

Admittedly, going to a monthly gathering represented yet one more thing on our crammed-to-capacity calendar and it meant the added headache of loading our entire crew (and about two dozen pacifiers) in our wretched minivan, but the companionship engendered and the therapy provided once we arrived made the endeavor well worth the effort.

You should make it your business to join such a group, immediately if not sooner.

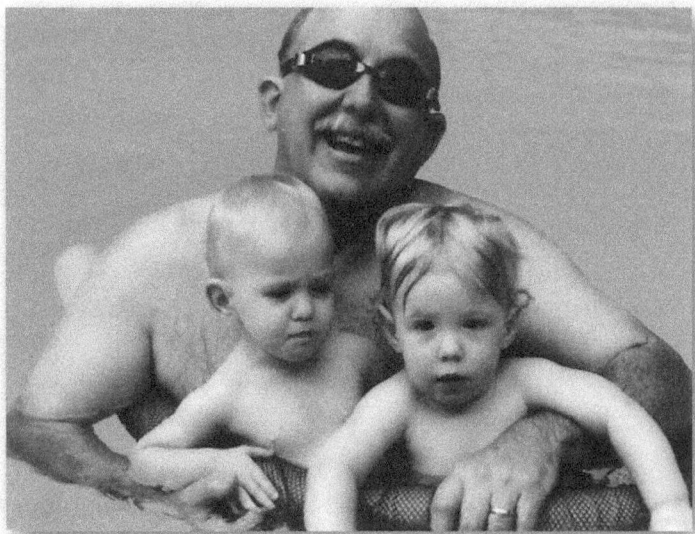

CHAPTER 7

Make it a Double.

Y ou're going to do it eventually—and you should. Hire a babysitter, that is. Like a lot of women, I was late to the party, thoroughly convinced that it wasn't necessary to take a break from mom duty like everyone else on the planet. I didn't deserve it. What's more, I believed I'd die of guilt if I actually picked up the phone and scheduled someone to care for my children. Once in a while. On a Saturday. For the tiniest wedge of time. Moreover, I felt it wasn't worth the aggravation (to prepare for) and the effort it would surely require to find a suitable candidate—someone who could live up to my impossible standards for a child care provider.

In my mind, the ideal stand-in would possess motherly qualities far beyond the norm, a Wonder Woman of sorts, sprinkled lightly with the essence of Mother Teresa and June Cleaver. Even when faced with the most challenging of situations, she'd manage them with both style and grace, juggling the demands placed upon her in spectacular fashion. And because I was slightly delusional, I felt that finding such a person was conceivable. I just needed to peruse a few hundred resumes and weed out serial killers and those prone to cannibalism.

Granted, the sitters we ended up employing were terrific. They were kind and compassionate as well as capable individuals, eager to do whatever was asked of them and more. Most, in fact, enjoyed watching our twins, swooning over them left and right. Naturally, upon my return a fair number felt compelled to share what a breeze the undertaking had been, citing examples of having extra time to wash the dishes, purge the refrigerator, empty the diaper pail, alphabetize my spices and sort the laundry BECAUSE THE BABIES ACTUALLY NAPPED leaving me to wonder why the universe hated me so.

In truth, I felt relieved that the sitters had had such wonderful experiences and only slightly envious that they were able to accomplish so much outside of the basics of baby wrangling. And because I had been a veritable disaster as a sitter myself, I was both inspired and amazed by their stories. As a teenager, I remembered caring for an adorable set of six-year-old twins along with their baby sister and elderly grandmother (despite my best efforts to block such horrors from my mind). Like a lot of teens, I felt a bit too sure of myself and never actually entertained the notion of something going wrong (read: fubar). Nor did I feel it was necessary to know how to change a diaper before I accepted the job. I'd learn that on the fly, I told myself. In hindsight, I had no business taking on such a responsibility and probably should have been banned from dog sitting anywhere in the state, never mind caring for someone else's children.

By the end of the evening, the baby's pants hadn't been changed (or even checked as I recall), but I *was* able to get most of the smoke out of the kitchen after nearly setting the house on fire.

Having this little gem-of-an-experience personally is perhaps what drove me to distraction when it came to the matter of selecting a sitter for my own children. I knew how quickly a situation could ~~become a shitstorm~~ deteriorate even under the best of circumstances. Thankfully, I overcame a lot of what was hindering my decision to move forward with the process, eventually accepting that I needed to rely on others from time to time. I needed to trust that everything would be okay—that no one would ride a tricycle off the roof or play in traffic. Probably.

To a large extent, I think what helped me move along on the continuum was the novel idea of hiring not one but two sitters at a time (usually twin sisters or a husband and wife team), making it a double. Once my husband and I discovered the benefits of such a practice, including the peace of mind it engendered within us, it became the norm. No longer was it something we did on a lark. It became standard operating procedure, and we never looked back.

Truth be told, I think the sitters preferred it, too. They could relax a bit, knowing that a safety net of sorts was there—another set of hands to rock and to soothe and to turn to when the task became overwhelming. Because invariably, it *would* become overwhelming. It was just a matter of time before the wheels would fly off with someone else at the helm. Needless to say, I felt infinitely better knowing that there were two levelheaded individuals there to support one another. And I think because the aforementioned sisters were twins themselves, they could fully appreciate what a challenge caring for two smallish beings at one time could be, which gave them all the more reason to hug their parents when they got home.

As a result, my husband and I spent more time enjoying our parenting reprieve and less time awfulizing every tragic scenario that could befall our charges in our absence. That alone was worth paying two sitters.

Years later, when our twins became preschoolers, we found that hiring two sitters at a time still contributed greatly to the preservation of our collective sanity. It benefitted our daughters, too, since our favorite twin teens went above and beyond to entertain them as well as stimulate their minds. Together they spent untold hours digging in the sandbox, pushing them on their swings, building with blocks and engaging with books.

But because of scheduling conflicts, we didn't always have the luxury of doubling up. We never compromised on quality though, always inviting the people who made it their business to actively involve our children. Some built elaborate blanket forts, enveloping the entire living room. *Oy.* Others baked cakes and endorsed the wearing of tutus throughout the land. One, an accomplished musician, even brought along her violin so that my dears might hear their favorite song roughly 846 times.

In the end, we recognized the importance of being able to count on reliable people to care for our twins. In the process, we developed an enviable list of individuals that we felt comfortable with. And because we allowed ourselves to be comfortable, guilt did not lead to anyone's untimely demise. As it should be.

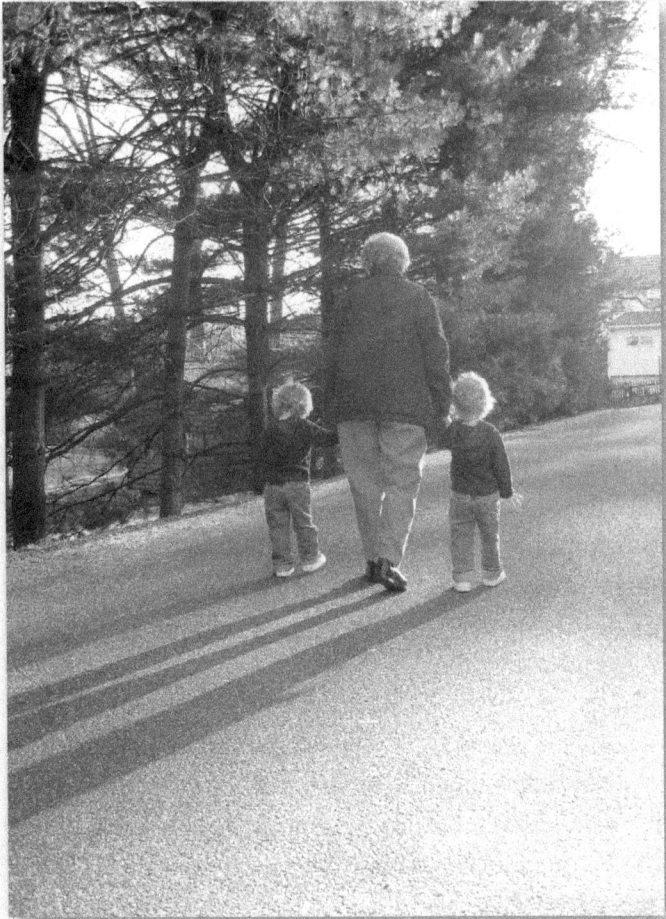

CHAPTER 8

Twin Fascination is Real. Brace Yourself.

Venturing out into the world with a set of infant twins is easily one of the surest ways to garner both attention and unsolicited advice from people you'll have absolutely no interest in speaking with. Like ~~flies to dung~~ moths to a flame, people will be drawn to your double stroller with crazy in their eyes, patently fascinated by the prospect of discovering answers to burning questions like:

"Have you figured out which twin is evil yet?"

"How'd you get pregnant anyway?"

"Sheez, I'll bet you were as big as a house! How much weight did you gain?"

"You don't seem busty enough to nurse two babies. How does that even work?"

"My Aunt Clara has twins and she told me that one shits more than the other. Is that for real?"

Needless to say, once my husband and I set foot outside with our duo, there was no escaping the throngs of perfect strangers who felt compelled to ogle and to probe and to satisfy their collective curiosities with a barrage of questioning that felt far too personal for my taste and more like being interrogated than anything else.

That said, the depth and breadth of insensitivity we encountered was mildly shocking and it didn't seem to matter where we traveled. To the park or grocery store. To the dentist's or pediatrician's office. To our beloved library or the dreaded mall. Somehow intrusive people managed to show up with disturbing regularity. Joy.

By the same token, there were lots of lovely people we stumbled upon who were courteous and tactful—people who fully recognized the importance of staying within the bounds of decorum (and at least 23.7 inches away from our dear children) as they approached our twin jogger, demonstrating the value of discretion and the beauty of restraint. Never mind that they, too, probably wanted to know whether my stretch marks would ever go away or if our babies were conjoined at the head. Because clearly they couldn't determine that from afar and would need to move closer for scrutiny's sake.

I guess I can't fault them for being genuinely intrigued. Twins are an anomaly to some extent, as are higher order multiples. That said, a herd of unicorns would probably attract less attention. Honestly, I can't imagine how presumptuous the vast majority of people must be when they happen upon triplets, quads or more—hovering like the pushy salesmen at the mall who insist upon slathering people's hands with pricey moisturizers, eager to shame them into buying. I only wish the strangers we encountered would've refrained from touching our twins and fingering the adorable little squeaky toys and pacifiers we tethered to them in an effort to keep them from becoming plagued with germs. So much for that pipe dream.

For a long time I wondered what possessed people who seemed to think that it made perfect sense to reach inside my stroller with their grubby mitts and paw at my children. People I'd never met. People who could've used a breath mint or two—and possibly some hand sanitizer. In the end, I suppose it didn't matter. Nothing horrible happened as a result of their apparent twin fascination. No one had been abducted or tattooed upon the forehead. No one's language development had been stunted due to an abundance of cooing, nor did anyone suffer the ill effects of having too many people smile at them in a given period of time.

Further, I had survived great multitudes petting the swell of my belly throughout my pregnancy (as inappropriate as that seemed in the produce aisle, where patrons were supposed to fondle melons, not the tummies of pregnant women). Surely, I would survive this, too. Never mind that I quietly freaked out inside my head, thoroughly convinced that the person now touching my child's bare toes had, just moments before, picked up and stroked a dead bird. Of course, I'd have no logical explanation for why that sort of thing might have occurred, but my mind would only allow me to fixate upon one tragic outcome: avian flu.

Worse though than those who encroached upon us physically, were those who refused to leave us without doling out a vat of parental advice. Granted, some of that guidance was utterly brilliant and we were grateful to have received it. Bear in mind, however, that we had a teenager and knew a thing or two about sleepless nights and the uncooperative nature of tiny humans. So it wasn't as if we were entirely inexperienced in the realm of childrearing, although at one point I felt as though giant signs hung from our double stroller and trendy set of backpacks.

PLEASE HELP US. OUR PARENTS ARE IDIOTS.

As true as that message might have been, the onslaught of uninvited counsel we received during that memorable first year was almost more than we could bear. There were people who thought we should dress them alike and people who suggested that would surely scar them for life. There were countless recommendations on diaper rash and sleep schedules, pureed vegetables and sunscreen—all of which would affect the likelihood of getting into college. Patiently, we listened to a gamut of opinions on dealing with colic, teething and fevers of undetermined origin as well as a host of strategies for inconsolable crying and the inevitable tantrums to come. Some folks were exceedingly passionate about cloth diapers, organic foods and the practice of swaddling while others felt compelled to share their views on the ever-popular breast versus bottle debate.

Looking back, I wish I had a dollar for every judgy remark or meddlesome statement I heard as a mom.

"Shouldn't those babies be eating solid food by now? Why aren't they in highchairs? My kids were eating slabs of bacon at that age."

"Aren't they too old for rocking? You'll spoil them."

"You don't let them sleep in your bed, do you? That's unsanitary."

"They *still* nap?" (or crawl or use pacifiers or suck their thumbs or drink from sippy cups, etc.) "They should grow up already."

"What is it with footie pajamas these days? Don't your children wear actual pants? And socks—why on earth aren't they wearing any SOCKS?!"

After a time, I learned to filter the advice from friends, family and others, keeping what I deemed useful and tossing the rest. I accepted the fact that I was a magnet for the pearls of wisdom people felt driven to share with me and considered that the aforementioned were truly caring and compassionate people, down deep. Their well-intentioned yammerings were just that. Well-intentioned.

CHAPTER 9

Romance for Dummies.

'm pretty sure having twins killed my libido. Dead. Not
completely dead—as if my love life deserved a eulogy and
would never ever return to this earth, but dead enough
that the likelihood of sex was at best remote. Never mind
romance. That required too much effort. And intellect. And
planning on my part. Not surprisingly, the demise of my
so-called passionate self had little to do with waning sentiment toward my husband and more to do with the perfect
storm of exhaustion and despair. Exhaustion due to being
perpetually sleep-starved. Despair due to a belief that my
exhaustion was likely permanent.

Those feelings were, of course, exacerbated by fear—
an overwhelming sense of dread woven into the fabric of
my being, which revolved around the very real possibility

of becoming pregnant again. There's nothing quite like the trepidation of being knocked up when one's world is already deemed unmanageable as it relates to the care and keeping of tiny beings. What's more, the thought of enduring another minute with impossibly swollen feet was almost unbearable.

However somewhere along the line (between the first tandem poopfest and the seventeenth episode of separation anxiety), I realized the importance of rekindling the intimacy that my husband and I once shared. We needed to get back to what drew us together initially—to remember why we fell in love in the first place. Doing so was not only vital to our relationship, but essential to our health and happiness as individuals. Translation: It would keep us from hurling our bodies from the nearest tall building or into the path of a freight train.

Interestingly enough, we weren't inclined to stoke the embers like most people. Unlike the swarming masses, we weren't especially moved by beautiful bouquets, chocolate-covered whateverness or sappy greeting cards intended to woo the socks off of the average schmuck. Instead it was the little things—the extraordinary moments wedged within our ordinary days—that made the biggest difference in the end. Like spur-of-the-moment back rubs, foot massages and that tiny window of opportunity sandwiched somewhere between giving our children baths and reading books—the one during which we fell into each other's arms for a fleeting yet delicious instant. Topping it off with a sensual kiss would then make us delirious with desire, yet entirely incapable of seizing the moment since we were nearly always dead tired, or feeding babies or ferrying them from the tub, their impossibly soft skin still damp and infused with traces of lavender and chamomile.

Likewise, on the nights when we didn't simply collapse into bed after our brood had finally succumbed to sleep, there was slow dancing in our darkened living room, the floor creaking in all the familiar spots, whispered I-love-you's shared in the wake of hearing each other's torrent of daily crises. There were handwritten words of encouragement and "Can't wait to hold you..." blurbages stuck to the bathroom mirror and orange juice container. Never mind the wildly unpopular PAY THE BILLS and EMPTY THE TRASH memos left on the counter, for there were hugs in the hallway (as we clambered over baby gates) and smooches at the kitchen sink (while we scrubbed baby bottles)—just because.

In addition, my husband and I would often take long walks together or sit on the swings in our back yard, dangling our feet in the dirt and catching up on the latest bits of chaos that had ostensibly threatened to consume us. Cloud watching while lying on our backs in the cool grass was another favorite way for the two of us to unwind. Ultimately, and almost without fail, the tension evaporated into the stratosphere. We held hands in our church pew as well—our twins draped over our shoulders like smallish sacks of flour, a distended diaper bag at our feet, the sanctity of our faith wrapped around us like a woolen blanket.

We shared the burden of household duties as well, which improved our relationship tremendously. Our favorite mantras were: "You wash, I'll dry." "You vacuum. I'll dust." And let us not forget: "You feed. I'll burp." On occasion, and well into our daughters' toddlerhood, our eyes would meet beneath the kitchen table as we crawled around on all fours, fetching errant peas and cereal they had flung far and wide from their highchair perches. His wasn't so much a come-hither look as much as a we're-in-this-together look, which spoke volumes to me about the depth of his love—and the hatred we collectively harbored toward the smooshed peas.

We were inclined to spoon each other in bed, too, although it rarely led to anything because, of course, we were either too spent or too crowded (i.e. a certain couple of somebodies were perfectly content to doze or breast-feed—between us). Once in a great while we were afforded the chance to cuddle on the couch, and if the universe allowed such a circumstance, we shared a torrid kiss-me-like-you-mean-it moment as my dear Romeo left for work. And although there was much to be said for spontaneity and the beauty of a quickie, the benefit of scheduling a standing date could not be denied.

Marking DATE NIGHT in big, bold letters on our calendar gave us something we could depend on and something we could look forward to with great anticipation. It represented a tangible reprieve from parenting—a delectable chunk of time specifically set aside for us. Naturally we were plagued by guilt each and every time we carried through with such an indulgence, but we truly needed to relax and reconnect as a couple. In a word, there was no substitute for "we time."

It didn't seem to matter how we spent the hours either, so long as we listened intently to one another, tried not to talk incessantly about our brood and gazed at each other until we could reliably produce either eye color or the current status of each other's nose hairs. Never mind that DATE NIGHT was often a glorified trip to the grocery store or a late night waltz through a home improvement store. One time I sat in a bathtub there and envisioned a scenario involving sultry music, the soft glow of candlelight and my husband's warm hands caressing my shoulders. In my mind, that qualified as a romantic interlude.

Stop laughing.

On a related note, just as we acknowledged the value of spending time together as a couple and one-on-one time with each twin, we recognized how important it was to carve out quality time for our oldest daughter, then a middle-schooler. Admittedly, there were mornings during which I found it impossible to drag my sorry self out of bed to see that she ate breakfast and was appropriately dressed for school—because, of course, my night had been horrendous, up and down nursing babies around the clock. More than once during that challenging first year, the poor kid was relegated to getting herself out the door and to the bus stop on time, with or without signed permission slips, gym clothes and her band instrument. On those unfortunate occasions, I never saw her until she returned in the afternoon. Mother-of-the-Year, I was not. And for that I felt enormously guilty and wanted desperately to make it up to her. As difficult as it sometimes was to fit family bonding time into our overloaded schedule, my husband and I tried to make it work—to make her feel as special as possible, given that we were beyond the point of fatigued much of the time.

Though having twins definitely changed the landscape of our love life (as well as family life), we discovered that that wasn't necessarily a bad thing. It was simply unfamiliar

terrain. The flame was still burning, but not any less bright-
ly or with diminished intensity. It was just different. That's
all. Romance had come to be defined by anything and everything that made us feel loved and cared for. Things like
a perk-me-up message in my husband's bagged lunch or a
love note left on his pillow. Thoughtfully prepared snacks or
a milk shake surprise waiting for me in the fridge. A stack
of laundry, neatly folded and carried to its destination even
before I had the chance to tackle it. The trash, gathered and
hauled to the curb for removal prior to its appointed pick-
up time. It was stuff that we did for each other—stuff that
we did for love—stuff that, oddly enough, kept the spark of
romance alive and well.

CHAPTER 10

Get in Gear.

remember it well. I was in the thick of pregnancy as my husband and I were standing in the mall parking lot, peering into the back of our SUV as if someone had curiously filled it with whipped cream while we were shopping. In actuality, we were scratching our heads over the issue of how we would ever fit our new double stroller into the cargo bay and still have room in the seating area for a diaper bag, two massive car seats and possibly our children. When it became painfully obvious that doing so would be, at best, inconceivable, we came to the sad but accurate conclusion that we needed a bigger car—or perhaps a Conestoga wagon, minus the dust from the Oregon Trail.

Needless to say, we wrestled with the stroller there for what seemed like an eternity, bending and twisting it into every imaginable shape until its contorted frame screamed in protest, refusing to cooperate entirely. We kept thinking there had to be a way to cram it in there. I just needed to do some math. I remember contemplating that we could potentially strap it to the roof with really long bungee cords and a prayer, or perhaps tether it to the bumper with one of the toddler leashes we had purchased earlier in the day—the one that the sales lady had frowned upon because she thought it was cruel to put children on leashes. "They're not *dogs*, you know."

"At least I'll know where the little heathens are," I defended inside my head as I walked away, forcing a smile and gritting my teeth.

At any rate, we discovered that the stupid stroller wouldn't fit inside our SUV unless and until we folded down the seats. So we did just that and drove home, defeated. Or at least *I* felt defeated and slightly bitter because, of course, it meant that we'd have to do the unthinkable—buy a damned minivan. I can't begin to express my displeasure with the idea. In a word, I loathed the notion of schlepping around in an oversized heap, something that would eventually become a home for wayward French fries and smelly soccer cleats.

Frankly I wasn't buying the cheery television ads that featured ridiculously charming families traveling in vogue in their shiny, new minivans, romanticizing the experience as something akin to going on a cruise to the Bahamas. Nope. I wasn't swallowing that. I just knew that before long I'd be riding shotgun and find myself tripping over a collapsible playpen, falling flat on my face in the middle aisle as I traipsed back to the car seats in order to trim my kids' fingernails while they slept—because, of course, that's the only way they would tolerate such foolishness. Turns out, my premonition was spot on. How can anyone look dignified while staggering around inside the belly of such a beast, I ask. Needless to say, my cynical self was convinced that excursions in such a vehicle would spell the death of me.

Not surprisingly, after the stroller debacle and roughly 47 seconds later, we bought one. The van of my dreams it was not. On a positive note, however, said van was instrumental in transporting our family ~~and a shitload of buckets and assorted shovels~~ during a host of memorable beach vacations—many of which featured sand as an unintended keepsake. It also provided endless fodder for a humor column I began writing shortly after my twin daughters were born and long before their teen drama would surface. Indeed, so much of parenting meant that I would never run out of material. But mocking the van, along with the multitudes of paraphernalia we had to buy upon becoming parents, was beyond therapeutic.

in my family for decades and some dear friends loaned us a handmade cradle that had been in their family forever. Both items fit nicely in our bedroom for weeks on end until our daughters graduated to cribs, and eventually to toddler beds. Of course, it required two master's degrees, a less-than-specific instruction manual and a substantial amount of shouting to properly assemble said items, but that was beside the point. We got the job done and that was all that mattered.

Almost instantly we discovered that we needed two diaper pails in order to function in our two-story home. In that way we were able to station one on each floor, near the changing areas, resulting in less running around to deposit dirty diapers and wipes. And let us not forget the aforementioned car seats, without which we couldn't have escaped our home. Ever. Granted, they were immense and unwieldy, but they served us well for a very long time. Likewise, we found our baby slings and backpacks to be virtually indispensible—godsends that enabled us to manage the logistical nightmare that transporting twins inevitably became. I imagine that a pair of infant carriers would work well, too, although we preferred the type that allowed us to function hands-free and to have close contact with our progenies, limiting the time spent wailing because Yin or Yang wanted to be held ad infinitum.

On a related note, two creaky, hand-me-down rocking chairs (as well as a marvelous glider chair we received as a surprise) were essential to our sanity since they possessed an almost magical quality, putting our babies to sleep nearly every time we rocked them. A pair of highchairs was a necessity as well, once they could feed themselves and demanded a bigger venue for playing with their food. It wasn't long before we discovered the genius of facing the chairs together so that our twins could interact to some extent, almost guaranteeing six minutes of peace during family meals.

As our charges became mobile and their thirst for danger and exploration became unbridled, we found that two play yards (or sets of connectable fencing) were highly effective in securing their safety as well as protecting our valuables. Eventually, however, they engineered a way to scale the fence ~~as well as run with scissors~~, just as they mastered nearly every other attempt to childproof our home. As for baby gates themselves, I can't reliably recall just how many we ended up purchasing (thank God for price breaks!), but I can safely say that they were a good investment. Without them, I fear my husband and I would've been certifiable.

Looking back, there were lots of things in terms of baby gear that we *didn't* need to duplicate. For instance, one activity center seemed to be plenty, as did a single doorway bouncer and activity gym. Of course, there was no need to have two twin strollers (unless one was all-terrain and the other was not). Nor was it necessary to have two infant bathtubs, twin bouncers or nursing pillows. However, we *did* use two swings, a pair of multipurpose playpens and two changing tables, although I could envision getting along with only one of each.

On a related note, even a Neanderthal would recognize the importance of stocking up on diapers, wipes, bath supplies and baby formula—instead of operating in crisis mode upon discovering that we had run out of some crucial item. Unfortunately, it took some time for our brains to evolve and there were, indeed, many days during which we operated in the aforementioned crisis mode.

Oddly enough, I'd advise purchasing three diaper bags—two small ones for traveling separately with just one child, and another large bag that would accommodate everything but the damned circus tent necessities for both twins. Naturally, I learned this the hard way, wasting a lot of time and effort to pack a bag on the fly. Because that's how I lived my life, it seemed. On the fly.

Likewise, I would suggest investing in three baby books—an individualized gem for each child to cherish upon adulthood, and one that highlights the entire twin experience—for parents to treasure a lifetime. After roughly three years ~~when I finally came up for air~~, I greatly enjoyed thumbing through said tome, which documented the beautiful mess that our first year had been. Honestly, it was such a blur I'm not sure that I would've remembered everything with the same degree of clarity had I not tangibly captured and compiled such a wealth of memories. Even as feebleminded as I was, living at the intersection of dazed, confused and slightly unhinged, I managed to spare enough minutes a week to record milestones, to craft personalized letters to each daughter and to snap a profusion of priceless photographs, all included therein. In a word, it was like filling a time capsule that I planned to revisit when my eyes could focus properly—at a time when I would become a different kind of mom: maker of sandwiches, applier of sunscreen and gracious recipient of dandelions.

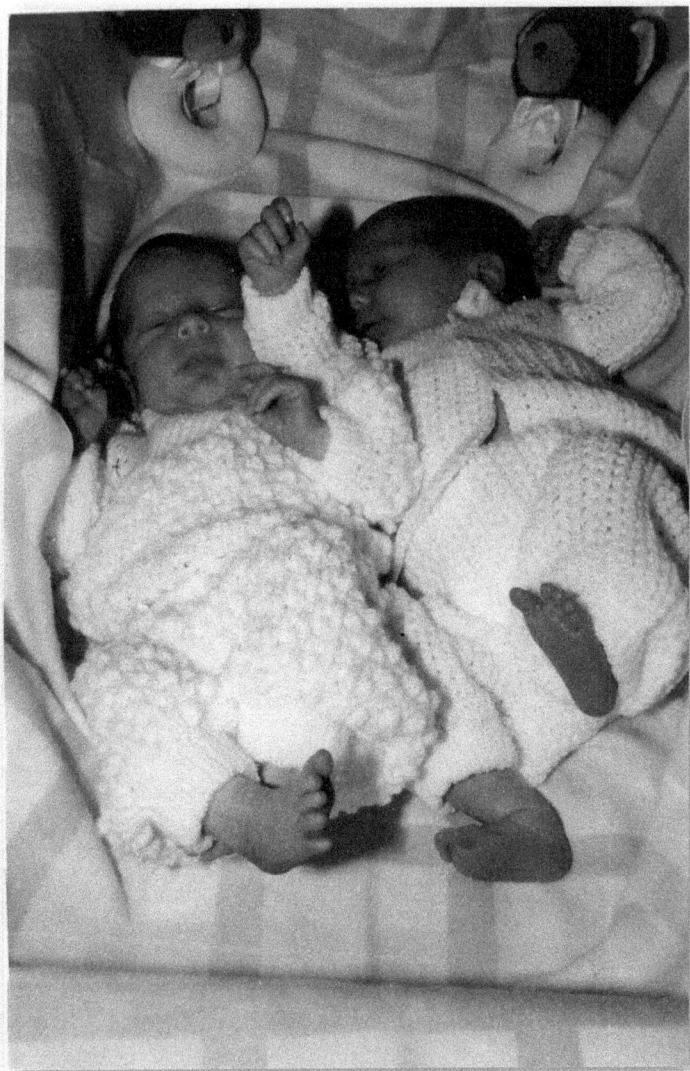

Epilogue

While it's true the term "motherhood" is a simple collection of 10 letters, specifically arranged for ease of pronunciation, it is suggestive of so much more. In sum, I regard it as a wholly intangible, behemoth-like affair that effectively upended all that I thought I knew about life as a decidedly callow 20-something. Needless to say, the experience continues to shape and mold me, schooling me day and night in the curious ways and means of children, wowing me with the inherent remarkableness of the aforementioned creatures and rendering me forever changed as an individual. As it should be, I suppose. That said, here's how I spell motherhood.

M Motherhood is a *messy* beast-of-a-thing—with its suffocating mass of sippy cups and sidewalk chalk, lemonade and lunch boxes, bicycles and building blocks. Never mind the ubiquitous nature of stuffed animals and the profusion of refrigerator-worthy masterpieces that inhabit our homes, marking time as our progenies progress along the winding path of childhood. And let us not forget all the lovely shades of gray with which we must contend: the tangled complexities of teens, the relentless questioning of toddlers and the soft underbelly of the headstrong child—the one we try desperately to govern without stifling. Indeed, motherhood is a messy business.

O Motherhood is *overwhelming* to be sure—a seemingly insufferable, plate's-too-full collection of moments that, when taken together or viewed within the prism of the unattainable ideal, beat us into submission, the thrum of parental failure ringing in our ears. That said, there's nothing quite like comparing oneself to the façade of perfection—holding our harried selves up against those who appear to be getting it right, the moms who keep all the plates spinning as if flawless extensions of themselves.

T Motherhood is *timeless*—an eternal post to which we are assigned, willing or not. From the moment our writhing infants, ruddy-faced and wrinkled, are placed upon our chests, motherhood begins in earnest. And although our parent/child relationships shift and season over time, they remain inextricably woven within the fabric of our lives.

Not even death can end the appointed role, as a mother's counsel is sought long after she has been eulogized.

H   Motherhood is a *humbling* experience. Ask anyone who has ever faced the stinging truth as it relates to intolerance and hypocrisy—delivered by a six-year-old, no less, soundly putting those who ought to know better in their respective places. So often kids eclipse our academic abilities, too, reminding us how important it is to embrace change. Never mind that every fiber of our being screams in protest. Moreover, becoming a parent means a humbling loss of identity to some extent, punctuating the uncertain nature of our so-called significance in certain circles. We are simply So-and-So's mom now—maker of sandwiches, applier of sunscreen, gracious recipient of dandelions. But somehow the title feels right, as does finding a pretty vase for the dandelions.

E   Motherhood is *edifying* in that literally every day we learn something new—most of which is harvested from conversations at the dinner table or at bedtime, from diaries that beckon unremittingly or from tiny notes we discover wadded up in someone's pants pocket. We spend a lot of time watching, too, realizing that our mothers were right all along. Children will, indeed, cut their own hair, shove peas up their noses and breach late night curfews to test both boundaries and our resolve. Arguably, the lessons of motherhood never truly end.

R   Motherhood is *real*. Good, bad or indifferent, it is palpable, inimitable and exceedingly enlivening. It is the stuff from which memories are made and so much purpose is derived.

H   Motherhood delivers nothing less than a *heady* rush—an intoxicating dose of awe wrapped in the sheer rapture of having had a hand in creating life, not to mention having been called upon to shape one or more future citizens of this world. Mothers are, without question, difference-makers.

O   Motherhood makes us swell with *omnipotence* now and again—a grand and glorious surge of I'M THE MOM, THAT'S WHY sort of sway that leaves us feeling all-powerful, if only fleetingly. But nothing makes us puff up more than hearing censure as priceless as, "Dad, did you get Mom's permission to do that? She's the Rule Captain, you know."

O   With motherhood comes *obsession*. And spiraling panic. And unfounded fear. And, of course, debilitating worry over that which will probably never occur anyway. In sum, we fret about bumps and bruises, unexplained rashes and fevers that strike in the dead of night…about report cards and recklessness, friends we cannot hope to choose and fast cars that will whisper to our charges, inevitably luring them within, despite our best efforts to forbid such foolishness.

D   Motherhood is *delicious*—a profoundly gratifying slice of life we would do well to savor. Never mind its patented swirl of disorder and wealth of doubts, fears and impossible demands. Indeed, motherhood threatens to swallow us whole, while at the same time allowing us to drink in its goodness, gulp by gulp.

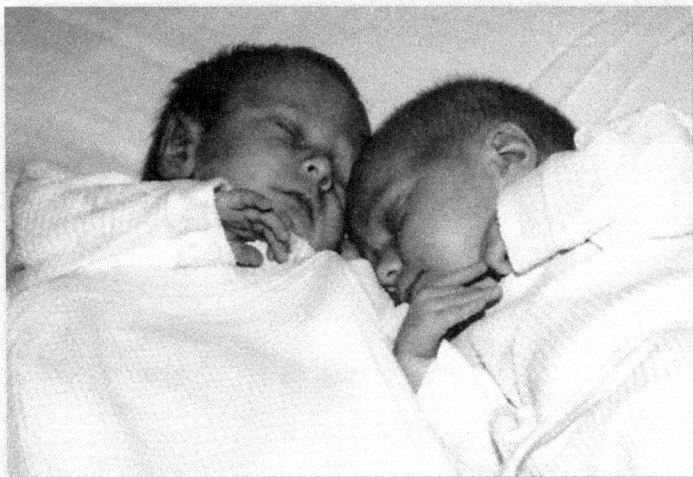

DELIVERANCE QUIZ

1) The enormity of your midsection most closely resembles
   a) Saturn b) The Hindenburg c) a Macy's Thanksgiving Day Parade balloon d) the remnants of something beautiful because it was integral in the creation of your children e) a walrus that swallowed a small city

2) "Find your tribe" means you should look for
   a) Apaches b) Iroquois c) tepees d) smoke signals e) a Parents of Multiples Support Group

3) If your babies nap you should
   a) begin stripping wallpaper b) clean the muck out of your gutters c) take a nap also d) alphabetize your cereal boxes e) bathe the family dog

4) As a new parent of twins it's easy to forget the importance of
   a) taking time for yourself b) sending your cat to culinary school c) tying your dog's sneakers in double knots d) playing tiddlywinks e) yodeling

5) When life becomes patently unmanageable with respect to handling the day-to-day insanity of rearing twins you would be wise to
   a) hide in a closet till they enter the sixth grade b) ask trustworthy friends or family for help c) suffer in silence d) run far, far away and leave no forwarding address e) commit hari kari

6) Two sitters are better than one because
   a) you can't play Rock-Paper-Scissors alone b) it makes the job of caring for twins more manageable, thereby creating a safety net of sorts c) double dutch jump rope can happen d) they're twice as likely to teach your children to play poker e) it takes two to tango

7) Putting your twins on the same schedule is important because
   a) the alternative is ugly b) having both babies on the same schedule makes life indescribably easier

    c) it's the only way you'll ever accomplish any-
thing outside of baby wrangling d) you'll actually be able to catch your breath e) all of the above

8) Now that you have twins, you'll probably need to
invest in
    a) a lot of baby gear to help engage, entertain and
transport your brood in a safe manner b) a cov-
ered wagon c) a live-in therapist d) six nannies
e) sedatives

9) Individuals who are fascinated with your twins are
probably
    a) aliens from outer space b) IRS agents c) people
completely taken by your wondrous creation d)
the paparazzi e) stalkers

10) With regard to your relationship with your spouse,
don't forget to nurture
    a) the dysfunction in your home b) your passion
for using the silent treatment c) your ability to
slather guilt with wild abandon d) the romance
you share e) your excellent nagging skills

DELIVERANCE QUIZ ANSWERS

1) d   2) e   3) c   4) a   5) b   6) b   7) e   8) a   9) c   10) d

Planet Mom: It's where I live, mastering the art of defective parenting. Spectacularly.

Join me there at www.melindawentzel.com
www.twitter.com/PlanetMom
www.facebook.com/NotesfromPlanetMom

About the Author

Melinda L. Wentzel, aka Planet Mom, is an award winning slice-of-life/humor columnist and freelance writer whose primary objective is to keep mothering real on the page while maintaining some semblance of sanity on the home front. She and her husband reside in the Northeast with their twin daughters, two pampered dogs and self-absorbed cat. Learn more at www.melindawentzel.com, follow her on Twitter at www.twitter.com/PlanetMom, read her spiel in the *Webb Weekly* at www.

webbweekly.com (*Notes from Planet Mom*) or find her on Facebook at www.facebook.com/NotesfromPlanetMom to share your in-the-trenches parenting moments.

It's not as if we didn't have a chance to consider what a life-changing event having multiples would be; it's just that we hadn't fully wrapped our minds around the embarrassment of gear it would require to outfit our brood from birth through college—imbeciles-in-training that we were. Becoming equipped as parents to handle two babies at once meant breaking the proverbial bank—both financially and psychologically, which, down the road, was sort of like stepping on toys in the middle of the night PRACTICALLY ANYWHERE in our household. It was a hazard of the trade. And immeasurably painful.

Thankfully, though, our lives were blessed with incredibly generous friends and family—people who stumbled over themselves to help us prepare for what was to come, knowing full well that we'd need two of almost everything. Obviously we required two cribs and a double dose of the respective bedding. Shopping for such an animal was a supreme challenge since I struggle mightily with indecision and because there were legions of pretty designs and patterns to choose from. Picking out insanely adorable mobiles, however, was my favorite part of the excursion and something I could handle despite my gross limitations.

Logically, it followed that a lovely pair of bassinets or cradles would be in order and it was my job to find them. We were fortunate enough to use a bassinet that had been